Unlocking the Secrets of Science

Profiling 20th Century Achievers in Science, Medicine, and Technology

Enrico Fermi and the Nuclear Reactor

John Bankston

Mitchell Lane
PUBLISHERS

PO Box 196 • Hockessin, Delaware 19711
www.mitchelllane.com

Unlocking the Secrets of Science

Profiling 20th Century Achievers in Science, Medicine, and Technology

Luis Alvarez and the Development of the Bubble Chamber
Marc Andreessen and the Development of the Web Browser
Oswald Avery and the Story of DNA
Frederick Banting and the Discovery of Insulin
Christiaan Barnard and the Story of the First Successful Heart Transplant
Tim Berners-Lee and the Development of the World Wide Web
Chester Carlson and the Development of Xerography
Wallace Carothers and the Story of DuPont Nylon
Francis Crick and James Watson: Pioneers in DNA Research
Jacques-Yves Cousteau: His Story Under the Sea
Raymond Damadian and the Development of the MRI
Gerhard Domagk and the Discovery of Sulfa
Paul Ehrlich and Modern Drug Development
Albert Einstein and the Theory of Relativity
Willem Einthoven and the Story of Electrocardiography
Philo T. Farnsworth: The Life of Television's Forgotten Inventor
Enrico Fermi and the Nuclear Reactor
Alexander Fleming and the Story of Penicillin
Henry Ford and the Assembly Line
Robert Goddard and the Liquid Rocket Engine
Otto Hahn and the Story of Nuclear Fission
William Hewlett: Pioneer of the Computer Age
Godfrey Hounsfield and the Invention of CAT Scans
Edwin Hubble and the Theory of the Expanding Universe
Robert Jarvik and the First Artificial Heart
Willem Kolff and the Invention of the Dialysis Machine
Barbara McClintock: Pioneering Geneticist
Lise Meitner and the Atomic Age
Joseph E. Murray and the Story of the First Human Kidney Transplant
Linus Pauling and the Chemical Bond
John R. Pierce: Pioneer in Satellite Communications
Charles Richter and the Story of the Richter Scale
Sally Ride: The Story of the First American Female in Space
Edward Roberts and the Story of the Personal Computer
Wilhelm Roentgen and the Discovery of X Rays
Jonas Salk and the Polio Vaccine
Edward Teller and the Development of the Hydrogen Bomb
Selman Waksman and the Discovery of Streptomycin
Robert A. Weinberg and the Search for the Cause of Cancer
Stephen Wozniak and the Story of Apple Computer

Enrico Fermi and the Nuclear Reactor

Printing   1   2   3   4   5   6   7   8   9   10

Library of Congress Cataloging-in-Publication Data
Bankston, John, 1974-
     Enrico Fermi and the nuclear reactor/John Bankston.
          p. cm. — (Unlocking the secrets of science)
     Summary: Examines the life of the Nobel-Prize-winning Italian physicist who, among other achievements, developed the world's first nuclear reactor as part of the effort to create the first nuclear bomb.
     Includes bibliographical references and index.
     ISBN 1-58415-184-6 (lib. bndg.)
     1. Fermi, Enrico, 1901-1954—Juvenile literature. 2. Nuclear reactors—Juvenile literature. 3. Physicists—Italy—Biography—Juvenile literature. [1. Fermi, Enrico, 1901-1954. 2. Nuclear reactors. 3. Nuclear physicists. 4. Scientists. 5. Nobel Prizes—Biography.] I. Title. II. Series.
     QC16.F46 B36 2003
     530'.092—dc21   2002014640

ABOUT THE AUTHOR: Born in Boston, Massachussetts, **John Bankston** began publishing articles in newspapers and magazines while still a teenager. Since then, he has written over two hundred articles, and contributed chapters to books such as *Crimes of Passion,* and *Death Row 2000,* which have been sold in bookstores across the world. He has written more than three dozen biographies for young adults, including *Francis Crick and James Watson: Pioneers in DNA Research, Robert Goddard and the Liquid Rocket Engine,* and *Alexander Fleming and the Story of Penicillin* (Mitchell Lane). He has worked in Los Angeles, California as a producer, screenwriter and actor. Currently he is in pre-production on *Dancing at the Edge,* a semi-autobiographical screenplay he hopes to film in Portland, Oregon. Last year he completed his first young adult novel, *18 to Look Younger.* He currently lives in Portland, Oregon.

PUBLISHER'S NOTE: In selecting those persons to be profiled in this series, we first attempted to identify the most notable accomplishments of the 20th century in science, medicine, and technology. When we were done, we noted a serious deficiency in the inclusion of women. For the greater part of the 20th century science, medicine, and technology were male-dominated fields. In many cases, the contributions of women went unrecognized. Women have tried for years to be included in these areas, and in many cases, women worked side by side with men who took credit for their ideas and discoveries. Even as we move forward into the 21st century, we find women still sadly underrepresented. It is not an oversight, therefore, that we profiled mostly male achievers. Information simply does not exist to include a fair selection of women.

Contents

A Nobel prize-winning physicist, Dr. Arthur Holly Compton assisted with the quest to build a nuclear reactor. His coded messages to U.S. government officials let them know how the atomic race was going.

Chapter 1
A New World

It was the peak of World War II when the message was sent.

"The Italian navigator has set foot in the new world," Professor A.H. Compton told the U.S. government's Office of Scientific Research.

"And how are the natives behaving?" asked James B. Conant on the other end.

"Very well," Compton replied.

Very well, indeed. The message was a code—it had to be, for on that December day in 1942 the United States had just pulled ahead in a race with Nazi Germany. The finish line would be the most dangerous weapon known to man; its use would help end one of the most destructive wars mankind had ever fought. On the last month of the year, an Italian physicist had constructed the first nuclear reactor, an important step toward assembling an atomic bomb. It was a step clouded in secrecy, but it was a natural progression from discoveries that had been made centuries before.

The study of matter and energy and the way the two interact is a branch of science known as physics. Physics seeks to explain what was once inexplicable—everything from why objects fall the way they do to how the smallest substances behave. In many ways, the first modern physicist was Galileo Galilei. During his life, from 1564 to 1642, the Italian mathematician conducted experiments that paved the way for centuries of scientific progress. Improvements to two of his inventions, the telescope and microscope, increased the power of these instruments and altered the way people viewed their world.

But by the 19th century, even the most powerful tools were not strong enough as scientists gave serious consideration to forces people could not see. Theories developed about light, gravity, and minuscule objects called atoms. Although the tiny atom was first described by Greek philosopher Democritus around 400 B.C., the study of atoms would not take place in earnest for over two thousand years. By the late 1800s and early 1900s, the focus was on increasingly smaller bits of matter called subatomic particles.

The word *atom* comes from the Greek *atomos,* which means "that which cannot be split." Democritus' idea that atoms were "indivisible"—so small they could never be divided—went unchallenged until near the dawn of the 20th century.

In the early 1800s, English chemist John Dalton published papers describing atomic behavior. His theories became widely accepted. Moving beyond Democritus, Dalton said all atoms of the same element such as iron, gold, or oxygen are alike, and atoms of different elements are different. Since then many of Dalton's theories have been proven correct.

His belief that atoms could not be changed or divided into smaller particles would later be disproved. Atoms *could* be divided or split; the proof of this theory would drive the work of scientists well into the 20th century.

Modern-day scientists usually either write theories or conduct experiments. But in the early 1900s, one man did both. He was born in Italy, the same country as Galileo. By then, however, Italian physics was in a state of decline, and Germany and the United States led the way in research and development. By fighting the prejudices of an older generation toward the science of the day, this man helped change the fate of science in his country. By fighting the prejudices of his nation, he helped change the world. This man faced persecution because of his wife's religion, which put his science and their lives in jeopardy. In the end, he and his wife came to the United States, where he helped to craft a device that won a war and provided an energy supply for generations. His name was Enrico Fermi.

As a child, Enrico Fermi lived his life in his brother's shadow. He found his strength in books on mathematics and physics. Years later, he was still painfully shy but success as a physicist slowly gave him confidence.

Chapter 2

So This is Growing Up

When he was a baby, Enrico Fermi did not live with his parents. This was normal. In early 20th century Italy, middle-class parents sent their children to a wet nurse, a woman in charge of infants, breastfeeding them and caring for them until they were weaned, or eating solid foods. Enrico was two and a half years old before he came home.

Enrico Fermi was born on September 29, 1901, in Rome, Italy. His father, Alberto, was a hard worker whose intelligence made up for his lack of a high school diploma. He rose in authority at the Italian railroad office, but he was 41 and recently transferred to the head office in Rome before he felt secure enough to start a family. Alberto married 27-year-old, Ida, who had been a teacher.

Young Enrico ventured from his wet-nursing experience to a household that valued learning, education, and achievement. Enrico would excel at all of them.

Enrico was the baby of the family, the youngest of three. His sister, Maria, had been born in 1899. Enrico was painfully shy—reading and studying were easy, making new friends was difficult. Fortunately, Enrico's brother, Giulio, just one year his senior, was outgoing and confident. He made sure Enrico had friends. A photo from that time illustrates the children's different ways of facing the world: Maria stands at the side, one hand on her hip, her face determined. Giulio is at the edge of the frame, but Enrico is tight beside him, holding his brother's hand, gazing fearfully at the camera.

The two brothers endured some sibling rivalries, but because they'd been born so close together, they behaved almost like twins. They shared everything. Together they built tiny electric motors and studied the power of electricity. Airplanes were a new and exciting invention; the two spent hours drawing their own "flying machines."

When Enrico was seven, the Fermis moved to an apartment at Via Principe Umberto 133, which was closer to Alberto's job at the railroad station. Although the rooms were spacious and the new house offered an indoor toilet, there was no bathtub or hot running water. Baths were taken in a small portable tub, the water left in it overnight and "warmed" to room temperature. When the apartment was especially chilly, the water would be heated on the stove. Their new home was always cold—so cold Enrico would later describe sitting on his hands and turning the pages of a book he was studying with his tongue. He didn't mention whether this method ever led to any paper cuts!

By the fall of 1911, Enrico was studying hard at the local middle school. According to his friend Emilio Segrè, he was at the top of his class, a boy who excelled at every subject—math, history, and Italian in the beginning; physics, Latin, and Greek later on. Besides being an academic star, Enrico played soccer and swam competitively.

By his early teens, Enrico could never learn enough at school. He and his brother would spend hours strolling through the stalls of books at Campo dei Fiori, a local outdoor market. There they would select a variety of used books. One volume on physics and mathematics was written in Latin, but Enrico was so absorbed by the subject he barely noticed. He wasn't exactly a scholar in that particular language, but the teenager was fast becoming fluent in the language of mathematics.

Enrico's life was blessed. His parents were loving and took good care of him. He had a passion for physics and knew it was something he could make his life's work.

In 1915, Enrico's pleasant life disintegrated.

Giulio had an abscess, basically a small pimple, in his throat. Removing it would be a fairly simple matter. However, something went tragically wrong during the operation, and he died from the anesthesia.

The loss was indescribable. Giulio was the oldest boy, a place of tremendous honor and responsibility in Italian families nearly a century ago. He was Enrico's protector. Their mother, Ida, slipped into the deepest of depressions. Enrico felt like his whole world was falling apart. A few days later, he walked alone to the hospital where his brother had died. His parents didn't want him to go, but the young teen needed to see the place where Giulio had spent his last moments.

After his brother's death, Enrico became even more of a loner. Life had become unpredictable and painful. In the world of mathematics, Enrico found escape. Mathematics was precise, it was straightforward. Using mathematics, he could chart a predictable sequence of events.

Enrico missed the interactions he'd shared with his brother. He was grateful when another older boy, Enrico Persico, came into his life. Persico had been a friend of Giulio's, and now he and Enrico Fermi spent hours digging through the piles of volumes at the Roman bookstalls and discussing their contents. Persico would grow up to become a prestigious physics and mathematics professor.

At home, Enrico's mother was deteriorating, and Alberto would take lonely walks around the city. One day Enrico trailed his father from his job at the railroad office; after that their strolls became a habit. It was a good way for father and son to bond. Losing his oldest had been a tremendous loss to Alberto, but now he took a greater interest in his second son. The two discussed the boy's dreams and his scientific theories. Although Enrico was still in high school, Alberto was impressed by his child—impressed enough to introduce him to a coworker, a well-educated engineer named Aldolfo Amidei. Amidei became a brand-new resource for the teenager, who made good use of the older man's knowledge. Besides asking the man questions every time they met, he was also able to borrow Amidei's old college textbooks. Amidei wondered how much someone Enrico's age would gain from such advanced works, but his skepticism disappeared when Enrico began quoting theories from geometry and trigonometry texts. Enrico completed the 200 problems in a geometry book, some of which even Amidei had given up on. Later the boy returned a borrowed calculus text.

"I told him that he could keep it for a year or more in case he needed to refer to it," Amidei later wrote in a letter to Segrè. "'Thank you,' he said, 'but that isn't necessary; I'm sure I shall remember it. In a few years' time I shall know it still better and if I'm in need of a formula I shall easily be able to recall it.' Indeed combined with his wonderful aptitude for science, Enrico had an exceptional memory."

As the two spent more time together, Amidei developed an interest in the boy's future. Rome possessed some fine universities, but for a young man with a scientific bent, there were few places better than the University of Pisa. Besides a top-notch education, the school offered dual enrollment with the local Normal School, which provided advanced teaching to future scientists. If he passed the rigorous entrance requirements, Enrico could be on his way to the finest education possible.

There was just one problem—Enrico's parents. Still mourning the loss of their first son, they didn't want to lose a second one, even if it was only to a school two hundred miles away. The Fermi household was filled with arguments in 1918, with Amidei pleading the boy's case—until he thought of a better solution.

Enrico would write the qulifying essay for the University of Pisa. If the school didn't accept him, then there wasn't any need to argue. If it did—well, they'd cross that bridge when they came to it.

Enrico's essay was on the distinctive properties of sounds. When Professor Pittarelli read it, he couldn't believe it wasn't written by a graduate student. After verifying that the paper was indeed written by a teenager, a boy preparing to graduate from high school, there wasn't a question about admitting him. In fact, Enrico Fermi at age 17 was almost qualified to teach at the college, let alone attend.

Albert Einstein was a patent clerk unable to land a teaching job when he developed theories which would completely change 20th century physics. His ideas were so complex, few understood them and soon a young Enrico Fermi would have to explain them to his much older professor.

Chapter 3
A Normal School

A teenager dreaming of a physics career could have picked quite a few places worse than the University of Pisa. The school had educated Galileo and given him his first job. The city's leaning tower provided the height the 16th-century physicist needed for his falling objects experiments. Yet in many ways the University of Pisa was resting on its history. The physics department had grown stale, the professors reluctant to accept many recent developments in the field. Enrico Fermi was fascinated by theoretical physics, a branch that thrived in the mind rather than in the laboratory. Unfortunately the school didn't offer a degree for theoretical physics, so it was a good thing that young Enrico was as talented at conducting experiments as he was writing about them.

While many of the courses he took were at the University of Pisa, the program in which Enrico was enrolled was conducted through the Scuola Normale Superiore, the Normal School, which had once educated teachers but had come to provide advanced training in the sciences to 40 of the best and brightest Italians. "Normal" students like Enrico were given free room and board at an ancient and ruined palace. While outside the building was impressive, inside the freezing temperatures were an unpleasant reminder of home. However, at night each student was issued a hot-water bottle; to Enrico this primitive method of keeping warm might have seemed the height of luxury.

After devoting so much energy to his entrance exam, Enrico must have been pleasantly surprised to discover how easy his actual studies were. Many of the classes covered books he'd already read. Passing tests was a breeze. Studying seemed unnecessary.

With too much free time on his hands, Enrico began filling his leisure time with the types of college high jinks familiar to many students today. He and his best friend, Franco Rasetti, formed the "anti-neighbor society," playing jokes on fellow freshmen, like locking colorful padlocks into students' buttonholes (and then "misplacing" the key). But when the pair set off a stink bomb during class, their jokes almost went too far. Enrico faced expulsion. After working so hard to get in, his dreams nearly went up in a puff of smoke. Fortunately, the school's physics professor stood up for the promising future scientist. Enrico took the lesson to heart, buckling down despite the ease of his studies.

Before the first year's conclusion, the professor approached Enrico. This time Enrico wasn't in trouble. The professor was. The older man, who had worked in the physics department for decades, was becoming overwhelmed by the scientific developments of the 20th century.

He wasn't alone. The professor had followed the advances in subatomic theory, but he could make little sense of it. By 1919, when Enrico began to educate his professor, scientists already had learned a number of important things relating to atoms.

They had learned that atoms aren't actually solid particles, but mainly empty space. Most atomic mass is in its central core, an area called the nucleus. As scientists later learned, this mass consists of two different particles, the proton and the neutron. Whirling quickly around the nucleus, like a fast-moving planet whipping in an orbit around the sun, are the electrons.

In the late 1800s, J.J. Thomson conducted experiments with a specially made glass cylinder called a Crookes tube. He experimented with the glow that occurred when electricity was shot from the negative metal plate on one side to the positive plate on the other.

Thomson learned that these "cathode rays are particles of negative energy. Atoms are not indivisible [they can be divided], for negatively electrified particles can be torn from their electrical forces. These particles are all the same mass and carry the same charge of negative electricity from whatever kind of atom they may be derived and are a constituent [a part] of all atoms."

Thomson wasn't just the first person to call these particles "electrons," he also disproved John Dalton's belief in the "indivisible atom." In 1920, just a short time after Enrico Fermi began helping his physics professor understand physics, Thomson's student Ernest Rutherford discovered that protons have a positive electric charge and electrons have a balancing negative charge. It was a student of Rutherford's whose work would be a major force in Fermi's post-school life. His name was Niels Bohr. Bohr would explain the motion of the electrons within the atom and the way those orbits relate to the atom's energy level. Another student of Rutherford's, James Chadwick, would prove the existence of the neutron.

Enrico's professor had lived though many of these amazing discoveries, but science is a lot like music. People usually enjoy the tunes they grow up with, the music that forms a background to their lives as young adults. But as they get older, they are often reluctant to embrace the music of the next generation. Of course, scientific theory is more complicated than pop music, but just like this year's chart toppers, the current scientific theory often disgruntles the older generation.

The professor was educated on Dalton's theory, and he'd studied the ways Thomson's work blew it apart. He understood Thomson, struggled with Rutherford, and, like many of his peers, was confused by Bohr.

However, no man's theories were as daunting and as confusing as those constructed by a patent clerk in Bern, Switzerland, during a single "miracle year" when the clerk was just 26 years old. His name was Albert Einstein, and by 1920, his difficult-to-understand theories were gaining acceptance. In fact, Einstein's theory of relativity was once jokingly described as a theory that was understood by only three people on the entire planet—counting Einstein!

Albert Einstein's explanation of his theory of relativity might have helped the confused professor. As Einstein explained it, "When you are courting a nice girl an hour seems like a second. When you sit on a red hot cinder a second seems like an hour. That's relativity." Einstein's theories of relativity attempted to prove a number of things—including that the speed of light is unchanging (and nothing can travel faster than light), and relativity occurs in a four-dimensional world of height, length, breadth, and time. Einstein's theories, explained in four articles published during 1905, revolutionized physics and the way the universe is viewed, just as Galileo's work had done three centuries before.

While Enrico Fermi couldn't completely explain Einstein's theories to the confused professor, his knowledge of physics led him to tell his old friend Persico, "At the physics department I am slowly becoming the most influential authority." Today, proof of this boast has been well preserved.

During the summer of 1919, Enrico went for a walk. An avid hiker, he often climbed the hills surrounding Pisa with friends like Franco Rasetti. This time, his only company was his notebook and his memory. When he reached the quiet summit, Enrico began jotting down all the physics he could remember. He scribbled notes about complex theories, he covered subatomic particles and the groundbreaking radiation research of Max Planck. Although Enrico used a pencil, Italian pencils of the time lacked erasers. He wrote entire passages without erasing or marking over.

The notebook has survived and is preserved at the University of Chicago. It reveals a teenager whose writings are not only incredibly accurate in describing the scientific theories of his time, but also uncanny in their predictions for the future.

For Enrico the present was idyllic, despite the incredible conflicts that had occurred not far from his classrooms. On June 28, 1914, the Archduke Ferdinand, heir to the Austrian throne, and his wife had been assassinated in Sarajevo. Suspecting that Serbia was the country behind the act, Austria, with the support of Germany, sent an ultimatum to Serbia. The response was hostile; Austria declared war on Serbia. Serbs allied with Russia, and Russian troops mobilized against the Austrian border. In the months that followed, countries that held treaties with the opposing countries were dragged into the conflict. From across the ocean, Canada joined the battle, and by 1917 the United States did as well.

In 1915, Italy sided with the powers that included the United States and formally declared war on Austria-Hungary, Turkey, Bulgaria, and finally Germany. The war's price was enormous. When it ended with the armistice on November 11, 1918, there were 37 million casualties; more than 600,000 Italian soldiers had lost their lives in battle.

Although the Great War, now known as World War I, devastated much of Europe, its impact on Enrico's life was actually positive. Graduate students had become soldiers, and even by the early 1920s the students who usually filled the graduate-level laboratory weren't there. By the time Enrico completed his sophomore year of college, he also completed his course requirements. At the age of 20, the young man was able to take full advantage of the facilities usually taken over by grad students. Although he surely felt the weight of so many lost lives, there was no denying that Enrico benefited from the tragedy, and there was little else to do but make the most of the circumstances.

He also began working toward his doctoral dissertation.

For his work, Enrico focused on X rays. While much of his passion lay with theoretical physics, in order to progress, he needed to focus on experimentation. His talents in the lab paid off.

Enrico's research drew from men like French professor Henri Becquerel, who had been developing a photographic plate coated with uranium salts when he saw silhouettes on the plate. The salts emitted radiation, which showed up on the plates just as light would have. These silhouettes represented the first time atoms could be "seen." It was also one of the first steps in X-ray development.

The aspiring physicist also looked at the work of a former elementary school teacher who lived in Poland during the 1890s, Marie Curie. Curie coined the word *radioactivity,* describing the radiation she had discovered in a number of different elements. Before Curie's experiments, scientists assumed uranium was the only element that emitted radiation. Curie discovered radiation in a new element, radium. Her work led to a variety of medical and scientific advances, from X-ray machines to atom bombs. Unfortunately, the radiation also killed her: She died of radiation poisoning in 1934.

In July 1922, twenty-one-year-old Enrico Fermi was awarded a doctor of philosophy degree in physics. It was time to return to Rome and apply what he'd learned to the real world. Unfortunately, the real world was about to get in his way.

Laura and Enrico Fermi look over the fruits of his labor. His life partner and sounding board for decades, Laura wrote a book, "Atoms in the Family" that provided valuable insights into Enrico's life for many biographers, including the author of this book.

Chapter 4

Love and Atoms

The Great War was over, and Europe began a long process of rebuilding. Across the continent, those countries most scarred by battle—France, Germany, the former Austria-Hungarian Empire, and England—worked to return to normal, to the way things were before the war. Millions of lives had been lost; whole cities, destroyed. Yet by the early 1920s, in the midst of reconstruction in countries that had lost the war, such as Germany, resentments over the terms of the surrender were already brewing.

In Enrico Fermi's home country of Italy, a new system of government was about to be adopted. The system is called fascism, and it is a form of government by which the country is run by a dictator, a single person who decides everything, from what newspapers may print and what the laws should be to how people may earn a living. It is the exact opposite of the democratic government of the United States.

Benito Mussolini was a writer who'd been injured during World War I. He claimed that fascism would be a better alternative for Italy than bolshevism, or communism. Although Italy had supported the Allies, which included countries like England and France, many Italian soldiers returning from the front lines were disgusted by the Treaty of Versailles, which they believed favored other European countries. The soldiers threw their support behind Mussolini and formed a group called Black Shirts. By the winter of 1922, Mussolini and his forces were gaining power, and the question was whether or not they would prevail.

Across town, Professor Orso Mario Corbino faced a simpler question. The former senator and current director for the Institute of Physics at Rome University was wondering whether or not to help Enrico Fermi land a job.

Professor Corbino had met Enrico a few months earlier, when the 21-year-old Ph.D. moved back in with his parents. Although in Italy single males (and females) often live with their parents until well into middle age, Enrico hated relying on the good graces of Alberto and Ida Fermi. Already his older sister had become a respected teacher of Latin and Greek; Enrico longed for a job offering that kind of stability.

Unfortunately there were few positions available for prospective physics professors. At the Italian universities most professors had tenure—lifetime employment—and jobs only became available when one of them retired or died. Since he'd graduated from the University of Pisa, Enrico managed to publish a few articles in some professional journals, but he had done little else.

Now, sitting across from Professor Corbino in his office at Rome University, Enrico listened politely while the director offered his opinion. The study of physics was declining in Italy, Corbino explained, and the real work was being done in other countries like the United States and Germany. The professor offered to get Enrico a fellowship in Göttingen, Germany, where Corbino believed the scientists were at the top of their game, doing research in physics ahead of everyone else. Enrico could work in such a facility for a year and then return to Rome.

Although he would have preferred to stay in Italy, Enrico accepted Professor Corbino's proposal. In the spring of 1923, Fermi joined the Ministry of Education in Göttingen. There he was all but ignored by the German scientists, who treated the young Ph.D. like a lab tech. Enrico's lifetime struggle against shyness became a huge battle.

The brilliant physicist lasted only seven months. He returned to Rome at the beginning of autumn and took a job teaching basic math to science majors at the University of Rome. It was not the best job for someone of Enrico's training, but he made the most of it. The most appealing aspect was it allowed him to stay in Rome, because if he hadn't stayed in Rome, he never would have met Laura, and he might never have fallen in love.

Laura Capon was the 16-year-old daughter of an officer in the navy. When Enrico met her, she was just a pretty teenager and he was the leader of a small group of friends. He chose her for his team during a pickup game of soccer on a Sunday afternoon.

"The young man had short legs, his shoulders were bent and his head was thrust forward," Laura later recalled in her book *Atoms in the Family.* "He shook my hand and gave me a friendly smile. It was hardly a smile, for he had very thin lips, but his eyes were laughing; they were set close together, leaving little room for his narrow nose, and in spite of his swarthy complexion they were blue-grey." As the pair competed against the others in soccer, young Laura quickly noticed, "His self-confidence was completely without vanity."

In many ways the confidence was an act. Inside, Enrico often felt like the shy kid he'd once been. Still, he projected a strong belief in himself and his ideas, and this is what was remembered of him, even more than his brilliant mind, as he took a brief fellowship in Holland and a position directing the studies of mechanics and mathematics at the University of Florence.

In 1926, Enrico got his break.

Professor Corbino had long been the young man's champion, because, as he often said, "only one or two men like Fermi appear in a century." Corbino created a chair, a head of department, for Enrico in theoretical physics. Only 24, Enrico was voted into the position by members of the Ministry of Education. Although most of them believed in him, one man didn't—the older department head of advanced physics. He believed Enrico should be working for him, not running his own department. After all, wasn't theoretical physics part of advanced physics? However, in science as in most things, the old must make way for the new: Enrico was placed in charge of his own department.

Enrico began in earnest assembling a small group of the best graduate students in physics. The team began radioactivity experiments to discover the power of the atom.

By 1927, Enrico's personal life was moving forward as well.

Laura and Enrico had been dating off and on for several years before she realized she was in love with the swarthy scientist. But would he pop the question?

Among his friends, Enrico was almost as legendary for his thrift as for his intelligence—he hated spending money. One day he confessed to Laura that he thought he'd spend some of the money he'd saved. On what? she asked. Oh, either a car or a marriage, he replied quite casually.

Laura was in Florence when a letter from Enrico revealed his decision. He'd bought a bright yellow Baby Peugeot, a sports car! Laura's heart broke.

Soon after, Enrico admitted he wanted both—a car *and* a bride. The two were married on July 19, 1928. They honeymooned in the Italian Alps and settled in a Roman apartment paid for by Laura's parents. They would eventually have two children, a daughter, Nella, who was born in January 1931, and a son, who arrived on February 1936. The couple named him Giulio after Enrico's brother.

Enrico was successful and young, and in many ways life seemed perfect. The only snag was that Laura was Jewish. This didn't bother Enrico, of course, but in Europe in the 1930s, the lives of many Jewish people were in jeopardy. Laura's was about to be one of them.

Although her mother Marie Curie may be better known, Irene Joliot-Curie and her husband, Frederic, conducted many important scientific experiments. When the couple caused an atom to give off radiation, it was an enormous step forward for nuclear physics in 1934.

Chapter 5
The Atomic Race

At his laboratory in Rome, Enrico Fermi was conducting experiments that would soon alter the atom. In Germany, a failed house painter named Adolf Hitler was embarking on political experiments that would alter the world. In 1923, Hitler had tried to overthrow the German government. After serving nine months in jail, he began gaining popularity and power. He professed the belief that Aryans (white, Protestant Germans) were a superior race, and that all others, especially Jews, should be expunged from Germany. He also claimed that he, as führer, was supreme and perfect. His beliefs became known as Nazism. By the late 1920s, many Jewish people had begun to leave Germany; some barely escaped with their lives. Most chose poverty over the type of life they feared they'd have in Nazi Germany. However, while Italy and Germany were beginning to form alliances, Enrico seemed too involved with his work to even notice. His focus was on smaller matters.

On January 15, 1934, the daughter of Marie Curie, Irène Joliot-Curie, and Irène's husband, Frédéric Joliot-Curie, caused an atom to give off radiation. When they bombarded its nucleus with alpha particles, the nucleus split. As the couple explained in a statement to the press, "For the first time it is possible to produce by exterior cause the radioactivity of certain atomic nuclei."

The couple's breakthrough inspired Fermi. However, he noted they'd used electrically charged particles and thought maybe an electrically neutral particle—consisting of neutrons alone, instead of protons and neutrons—would be better for the job.

That winter, Fermi and his graduate students embarked on the tedious task of determining which of the 92 known chemical elements would provide the longest burst of radioactivity.

"[N]eutrons were already known to be an efficient agent for producing some nuclear disintegrations," Fermi later explained. "As a source of neutrons in these researches I used a small glass bulb containing beryllium powder and radon."

In his experiments, Fermi was helped by old friends, including Amidei and Segrè. Still, it must have seemed like a long, cold winter as the group bombarded 91 elements.

And then they reached 92. Uranium. Its bombardment led to the discovery of two new elements, numbers 93 (neptunium) and 94 (plutonium). Fermi also learned that when he placed a barrier of paraffin in the way of the alpha particles, the effectiveness of the neutron was increased.

While Enrico's experiments continued, in Germany Hitler was the country's new leader, and soon anti-Semitic laws—laws against Jewish people—would be passed and brutally enforced. These laws would quickly reach Italy, and Laura Fermi.

In 1938, one woman's work complemented Fermi's and helped to usher in the "atomic age." Just as Fermi had been inspired by the research of Marie Curie, Curie's experiments inspired another woman, Lise Meitner, to pursue higher education. Meitner was one of the few women of the time to earn a doctorate, receiving her Ph.D. from the

University of Vienna. She worked with Max Planck, the developer of quantum theory, which holds that energy, like heat and light, is made up of separate units called quanta. But it was her work with a pair of Ottos—chemist Otto Hahn and nephew and physicist Otto Frisch—that led Albert Einstein to call her "the German Marie Curie."

Like Albert Einstein and Laura Fermi, Lise Meitner was Jewish. Soon after her experiments, she found that, because of her faith, her life was threatened by Hitler's policies. She remained in Austria until 1938, when Hitler invaded. Managing to escape to Sweden, Meitner worked with the Nobel Institute of Theoretical Physics.

Otto Hahn, her partner in discovering a new chemical element, protactinium, stayed in Germany. In late 1938, during experimentation with neutrons, Hahn and his assistant, Fritz Strassmann, disproved a fundamental atomic theory, one held as true since Dalton first proposed it over one hundred years before.

Neutrons, because they lack an electrical charge, can be "shot" into the nucleus of an atom like a bullet. In Richard Rhode's book, *The Making of the Atom Bomb,* physicist I. I. Rabi explains, "When a neutron enters a nucleus, the effects are as catastrophic as if the moon struck the earth. The nucleus is violently shaken up by the blow, especially if the collision results in the capture of the neutron. A large increase in energy occurs and must be dissipated and this may happen in a variety of ways, all of them interesting."

After bombarding a uranium nucleus with neutrons, Hahn and Strassmann thought they'd "chipped away" part of the uranium and produced radium. However, radium is separated from uranium by four atomic numbers—a distance that made such an occurrence unlikely. They knew from Curie's work that barium and radium were so close on the atomic scale that they were difficult to distinguish.

"There was nothing in the knowledge of nuclear physics to suggest that barium could possibly be produced as a result of the irradiation of uranium with neutrons," Hahn later explained in Ruth Moore's biography of Niels Bohr.

When Hahn sent a letter to Meitner, she replied, "Your radium results are very startling."

If he had been any other scientist, she would have assumed he'd made a mistake. But Meitner knew Hahn. She'd worked with him. She realized that the neutron hadn't just chipped at the nucleus of the uranium. It had split it in two! Atoms could be divided, even changed, and when that happened, an enormous energy release would occur.

In biology, when a cell splits apart, it is called fission. Lise Meitner, still working with Otto Frisch, decided to call this splitting of the atom "nuclear fission." She would also carefully calculate the potential energy release, relying in part on Einstein's theory of relativity. Despite the theory's complexity, it yields a very elegant and simple-looking equation, and probably the most famous formula in history: $E = mc^2$.

In this formula, E is energy, m is mass, and c is the speed of light. Einstein's formula showed that matter—or mass—is really bottled-up energy. Just a small amount of matter could release a tremendous amount of energy. This formula explains how our sun has been able to produce heat and light for billions of years. The constant nuclear explosions on the sun convert small amounts of matter into incredible amounts of energy. The formula's conclusions would also later be used to truly devastating effect.

When she finished her calculations, Meitner was astonished. She checked them again.

She'd proved it. A single gram of uranium, under the right conditions, could release as much energy as many pounds of dynamite. Hahn's discovery could lead to a weapon of unimaginable consequence.

And the Nazis knew about it!

That same year, Enrico Fermi learned he'd won the Nobel Prize in physics. The prize was an incredible honor, but it also gave the Fermi family a once-in-a-lifetime opportunity.

The prize would be awarded in Sweden. The Fermis would have an excuse to leave Italy, and not a moment too soon. For under Mussolini's control, creative people like scientists suffered the most. Members of Fermi's team had begun to leave. Enrico's position was even more dangerous because of Laura. Although Italy's Jewish population was less than one percent, many of the Jews there had been prominent businesspeople and politicians. Not only had the prime minister of Italy in 1909 been Jewish, along with a number of senators, but some of Mussolini's own men were Jewish. Despite this, in August 1938, Mussolini enacted laws that negatively affected Jewish people.

The Stockholm trip provided an escape for Fermi's family. They contacted the American embassy in Rome and made arrangements. On December 6, the Fermi family left Italy. They would not be back.

Enrico Fermi was a teacher as well as a scientist. For many years, his students at schools like Columbia and the University of Chicago were able to learn about the latest breakthroughs in theoretical physics.

Chapter 6
Reactor!

On January 2, 1939, Enrico Fermi arrived in New York City. He had a Nobel Prize, a teaching job at prestigious Columbia University, and a head filled with ideas. He'd need them.

Fermi and his new assistants began work quickly. Their goal was to take nuclear fission to the next level—creating a nuclear reactor. They used a form of uranium known as U-235. When its nucleus was split by a neutron, the U-235 would release energy and more neutrons, which would split more nuclei in a chain reaction. By building an "atomic pile" of U-235 and graphite and setting the splitting of the nuclei in motion, the neutrons would continue to split nuclei at increasing rates of speed in a sustained chain reaction.

With Germans like Otto Hahn hard at work on similar experiments, several prominent scientists visited Albert Einstein at his home on Long Island. They convinced him to sign a letter to the president of United States, urging him to develop a nuclear weapons program.

The August 2, 1939, letter to President Franklin Roosevelt explained that the results of "recent work by E. Fermi and L. Szilard," a scientist working with Fermi, could "lead to the construction of bombs. . . . A single bomb of this type, carried by boat and exploded in a port, might very well destroy the whole port together with some of the surrounding territory." The letter also warned, "some of the American work on uranium is now being repeated" in Berlin.

The letter was right about the bomb's potential. He was wrong about how it would be delivered.

Less than one month after Einstein's fateful letter, the German army invaded Poland. Overwhelmed by the superior force, the Poles were quickly defeated. Other countries, including France and Holland, would also fall, but it was Germany's invasion of Russia that led that country to begin developing their own atomic weapon.

As a new decade dawned, three countries—Germany, Russia, and the United States—were locked in a dangerous competition. The "winner" would be the first one to develop an atomic bomb.

By the fall of 1941, Fermi and his assistants had constructed a column of graphite and uranium for their atomic pile. Then they realized something important. The ceiling in the laboratory was too low to safely conduct the experiment. The experiment was halted.

Although not yet officially involved in the war, the U.S. government recognized the threat created by Nazi Germany. When the United States entered the war following a surprise attack on Pearl Harbor by German ally Japan on December 7, 1941, the effort to design an atomic bomb was already under way.

Code-named the Manhattan Project, the effort would cost over two billion dollars in less than four years. This was an enormous amount of money in the 1940s—more than the value of the entire automotive industry.

The Manhattan Project consisted of several, separate laboratories working toward a common goal.

In Oak Ridge, Tennessee, the uranium isotope U-235 was separated from less fissionable (and thus less explosive) U-238. This was done by using a calutron—a cyclotron from California University—which relied on an electromagnetic field to accelerate the uranium atoms in a circle and separate the isotopes.

On January 24, 1942, Fermi went to the University of Chicago to construct a nuclear reactor. Otto Frisch, Meitner's nephew, was leading this effort. The location for the world's first nuclear reactor was an odd choice—an unused squash court beneath the stands of the school's football stadium. There, at least, the ceilings would be high enough.

By then Enrico's home country, Italy, was at war with the United States. Because of this, Enrico was considered an "enemy alien." He couldn't travel by airplane. He had to check in with government officials regularly, and his every move was monitored. But his research was left alone.

On December 2, 1942, at 9:45 A.M., the atomic pile experiment—testing the first nuclear reactor—began. Four hundred tons of graphite, six tons of uranium metal, and fifty-eight tons of uranium oxide were used in its construction. Fermi observed from a platform over the pile as one of his assistants started the process. By 5:25 that night, their tests proved the chain reaction was beginning. The pile would release nuclear energy in a controlled way.

Of all the laboratories working toward the atomic bomb, probably the best known was the one in Los Alamos, New Mexico, which worked in partnership with the University of California. The lab was isolated and desolate when Fermi and his family arrived there in the summer of 1944. The climate may have been uncomfortable, but the lab offered him the chance to be part of the team building an atomic bomb. He was the team leader, heading up F Division—the *F* for "Fermi." Because of the fears that Germany might soon have their own atomic bomb, nearly every available scientist was put to work.

Germany surrendered on May 7, 1945. They never came close to building an atomic bomb. Japan, however, was still a threat, and the war, along with the Manhattan Project, continued.

On July 16, 1945, at test site Trinity, 200 miles south of Los Alamos, the first successful test of an atomic bomb was conducted. It was an awesome sight as a mushroom-shaped cloud blasted 40,000 feet over the desert sky, blinding light flashed below, and the ground shook violently.

The bomb was a success—the single blast was equivalent to more than 20,000 tons of dynamite.

Many of the scientists who viewed the test believed that if the Japanese could see what they had just witnessed, the war would be over. A number of them lobbied government officials to demonstrate the weapon's power over an isolated, unpopulated area of Japan. Surely once Japanese officials realized how powerful the weapon was, they'd give up.

Robert Oppenheimer, the head of Los Alamos, and Enrico Fermi disagreed with them. They spoke with President Harry Truman, explaining how a ground invasion could cost thousands of American soldiers their lives but a mere demonstration was too risky. Truman agreed. In her book *Atoms in the Family,* his wife Laura said, "Enrico did not think that for the physicists to stop their work would have been a sensible solution. Nothing is served by trying to halt the progress of science. Whatever the future holds for mankind, however unpleasant it may be, we must accept it, for knowledge is always better than ignorance." Since Enrico was alive when she wrote this, he most likely agreed with her assessment.

An atomic warhead was loaded into the bomb bay of the *Enola Gay*, the plane chosen to deliver this deadly cargo. On August 6, 1945, the plane flew over Japan, dropping the atomic bomb on the city of Hiroshima.

The destructive power of that bomb and the one that followed it at Nagasaki three days later vaporized buildings and instantly killed a total of over 150,000 people. Just as many would die later from illnesses caused by radiation.

The bomb worked.

Japan formally surrendered on September 2, 1945. The work at Los Alamos to develop a nuclear weapon was over. In 1946 Enrico Fermi returned to The University of Chicago, where he joined the faculty and became a U.S. citizen. At the time a number of scientists lobbied the U.S. government to put into place an organization, run by the nations of world, to oversee atomic energy. Fermi refused to join them; he felt the right country had the bomb and that the atomic energy program would eventually provide nuclear reactors for civilian use, providing energy to civilians just as atomic power had supplied bombs for the military.

However, Fermi did speak out against the work of a scientist he'd met at Columbia University, Edward Teller. The two had discussed the work of Teller's boss, George Gamow, who'd been examining how stars like our sun generate their energy. Gamow discovered that lightweight nuclei—such as hydrogen—will fuse and create enormous energy when subjected to high temperatures. Fermi wondered if this principle could be brought down to earth. Could an atomic bomb be used to create an even more powerful weapon—by exploding and causing the fusion of hydrogen, which would enormously increase the explosion's force?

After the war, however, Fermi saw little need for more powerful weapons and lobbied against testing a hydrogen bomb. The test went forward anyway.

Enrico Fermi spent the last nine years of his life in Chicago. In 1954 the Atomic Energy Commission gave him a Presidential award for his work. Within two years the award would bear his name. Today the Enrico Fermi Award is given for "exceptional achievement in the development, use, or production of energy," and winners receive $100,000. Edward Teller, Robert Oppenheimer, Otto Hahn, Lise Meitner, and Fritz Strassmann were all recipients in the 1960s.

Memorializing his name with this award was not the only way the world would honor him. On November 29, 1954, Enrico Fermi died of stomach cancer. The next year, American chemist Glenn T. Seaborg discovered a new element among the remnants of the first test of Teller's hydrogen bomb. He named it fermium.

Enrico Fermi Chronology

1901   Enrico Fermi is born in Rome, Italy, on September 29

1911   Enters middle school

1915   After brother Giulio's death, retreats further into world of physics and reading

1918   Is accepted at Pisa's Scuola Normale Superiore

1921   Publishes first scientific paper

1922   Earns Ph.D.

1923   Works at University of Göttingen, Germany, then teaches at the University of Rome

1926   Given newly created chair of theoretical physics department at University of Rome

1928   Marries Laura Capon on July 19

1931   Daughter, Nella, is born

1934   Conducts experiments to generate radioactivity

1936   Son, Giulio, is born

1938   Wins Nobel Prize in physics; leaves Italy

1939   Arrives in New York City; begins work on nuclear reactor at Columbia University; becomes involved in the top-secret Manhattan Project

1942   Moves research to University of Chicago; first reactor successfully operated on December 2

1944   Becomes U.S. citizen; moves to Los Alamos, New Mexico, to continue atomic bomb research

1946   Joins University of Chicago faculty

1954   Dies of stomach cancer on November 29

1956   Enrico Fermi Award established to award "exceptional achievement in the development, use, or production of energy"

Timeline of Discovery

1803 English chemist John Dalton introduces atomic theory.

1869 Dmitry Mendeleyev publishes periodic table of the elements.

1895 Wilhelm Roentgen discovers X rays.

1896 Henri Becquerel discovers uranium's natural radioactivity.

1897 Joseph John (J.J.) Thomson discovers the electron.

1898 Marie and Pierre Curie discover radium.

1900 Max Planck develops quantum theory.

1905 Albert Einstein publishes theory of relativity and his famous equation $E = mc^2$, the law of the equivalence of mass and energy.

1908 Ernest Rutherford and Hans Geiger invent radiation counter.

1911 Ernest Rutherford publishes theory of the nuclear structure of atoms.

1919 Ernest Rutherford discovers the proton.

1932 James Chadwick proves existence of the neutron.

1934 Irène and Frédéric Joliot-Curie split an atom using alpha particles.

1938 Otto Hahn and Fritz Strassmann split uranium atom.

1941 Enrico Fermi proposes H-bomb theory.

1942 In Chicago, the first chain-reaction nuclear reactor is tested.

1945 Nuclear fission bomb dropped on two cities in Japan, Hiroshima and Nagasaki, changing warfare strategy forever.

1946 U.S. Atomic Energy Commission is created.

1951 First atomic clock, which took two years to build, is fully operational.

1952 Hydrogen bomb is tested for the first time.

1954 USS *Nautilus*, the first nuclear-powered submarine, is launched. The world's first nuclear power plant is opened in Obninsk, Russia.

1974 Energy Reorganization Act establishes the Energy Research and Development Administration (now part of the U.S. Department of Energy) to oversee military use of nuclear energy and the Nuclear Regulatory Commission to oversee civilian use. These organizations replace the Atomic Energy Commission.

1979 U.S. nuclear power plant at Three Mile Island, Pennsylvania, suffers partial meltdown.

1985 IBM scientists use scanning tunneling microscope to see atoms for the first time.

1986 Accident at Soviet nuclear plant at Chernobyl kills more than 30 people outright and injures thousands.

2003 U.S. Navy turns its base on the island of Vieques over to the Department of the Interior, ending 60 years of military testing there. Among the toxic pollutants left behind are depleted uranium shells.

Further Reading

For Young Adults

Bankston, John. *Albert Einstein and the Theory of Relativity.* Hockessin, Del.: Mitchell Lane Publishers, 2002.

———. *Edward Teller and the Hydrogen Bomb.* Hockessin, Del.: Mitchell Lane Publishers, 2001.

———. *Lise Meitner and the Atomic Age.* Hockessin, Del.: Mitchell Lane Publishers, 2003.

Berger, Melvin *Atoms, Molecules and Quarks.* New York: G.P. Putnam and Sons, 1986.

Beyer, Don E. *The Manhattan Project: America Makes the First Atomic Bomb.* New York: Franklin Watts, 1991.

Hamilton, Janet. *Lise Meitner: Pioneer of Nuclear Fission.* Berkeley Heights, N.J.: Enslow Publishers, 2002.

Henderson, Harry. *Nuclear Physics.* New York: Facts on File, Inc., 1998.

Pasachoff, Naomi. *Marie Curie and the Science of Radioactivity.* New York: Oxford University Press, 1996.

Whiting, Jim. *Otto Hahn and the Story of Nuclear Fission.* Hockessin, Del.: Mitchell Lane Publishers, 2004.

Works Consulted

Boorse, Henry A., Lloyd Moltz, and Jefferson Hane Weaver. *The Atomic Scientists: A Biographical History.* New York: John Wiley, 1989.

Cooper, Dan. *Enrico Fermi and the Revolutions of Modern Physics.* New York: Oxford University Press, 1999.

De Latil, Pierre. *Enrico Fermi: The Man and His Theories.* New York: Paul S. Eriksson, Inc., 1966.

Fermi, Laura. *Atoms in the Family.* Chicago: University of Chicago Press, 1954.

Moore, Ruth. *Niels Bohr: The Man, His Science and the World They Changed.* Cambridge, Mass.: MIT Press, 1985.

Rhodes, Richard. *The Making of the Atom Bomb.* New York: Simon and Schuster, 1986.

Internet Addresses

"Enrico Fermi," Spartacus Educational
www.spartacus.schoolnet.co.uk/2WWfermi.htm

"The Enrico Fermi Award"
www.pnl.gov/fermi/index.html

"Enrico Fermi Institute," University of Chicago
http://efi.uchicago.edu/

"The Nobel Prize in Physics, 1938," Nobel e-Museum
www.nobel.se/physics/laureates/1938/

Manhattan Project Heritage Preservation Association, Inc.
http://www.childrenofthemanhattanproject.org/index.htm

U.S. Nuclear Regulatory Commission
www.nrc.gov/

Glossary

acceleration—rate of change of velocity.

alpha particle—a positively charged nuclear particle that consists of two protons and two neutrons. It is ejected at high speeds in certain radioactivity experiments.

atom—smallest unit that makes up chemical element.

atomic pile—a nuclear reactor, named for the first actual stacks of uranium and graphite used in the reactor.

calculus—a branch of advanced mathematics that involves continuously changing values.

chain reaction—the result of a neutron splitting an atom and releasing more neutrons, which split more atoms and release more neutrons, and so on.

Crookes tube—a type of vacuum tube developed to study X rays.

electron—a tiny, almost weightless atomic particle that contains a negative electrical charge and orbits around the nucleus of an atom.

element—a substance that is composed entirely of atoms of one type.

fission—the splitting of the nucleus of an atom.

fusion—the combining of two atoms to form one heavier atom.

isotope—a form of an element that contains a different number of neutrons than the usual form.

neutron—a particle, located in the nucleus of an atom, that has no electrical charge.

nuclear—being, coming from, or related to an atomic nucleus.

nucleus—the center of the atom.

proton—a particle, located in nucleus of an atom, that carries a positive electrical charge

radioactivity—process by which some elements give off particles and rays.

reactor—device that uses controlled nuclear fission to release energy from radioactive substances.

subatomic—dealing with particles smaller than atoms.

Index